Contents

Growing up in India

Mohandas Gandhi was born on 2 October 1869 in Porbandar, a small state on the coast of north-west India.

He was the youngest of four children, with one sister and two brothers. His father was Prime Minister of Porbandar. His mother was a Hindu who worshipped every day in the temple. The family's home was full of books about religion.

Gandhi went to the local primary school. He liked reading and writing, but could not learn the multiplication tables. He was too shy to talk to the other children.

Gandhi's mother was very religious at a certain time of the year she would only eat if the sun came out.

Famous People

MOHANDAS GANDHI
1869~1948

Christine Moorcroft

Magnus Magnusson

Christine Moorcroft is an educational consultant and an Ofsted inspector, who was a teacher in primary and special schools and a lecturer in education. She has written and edited several books on history and religion and on other subjects, including personal and social education, science and English.

Magnus Magnusson KBE, has written several books on history and archaeology, and translated many Icelandic sagas and modern Icelandic novels. He has presented major television programmes on history and archaeology, such as *Chronicle*, *The Archaeology of the Bible Lands* and *Living Legends*, as well as the long-running quiz series, *Mastermind*. He is currently chairman of Scottish Natural Heritage, the Government body which advises on environmental issues.

ACKNOWLEDGEMENTS

The authors thank the staff of Childwall Library, Liverpool, for their help.

Picture credits
Topham Picture Library: pages 5, 7, 11, 12, 15, 16, 18, 19
Camera Press: pages 6, 13, 17,

Published by Channel Four Learning Limited
Castle House
75–76 Wells Street
London W1P 3RE

© 1998 Channel Four Learning

Written by Christine Moorcroft and Magnus Magnusson
Illustrated by Michelle Ives
Cover illustration by Jeffrey Burn
Designed by Blade Communications
Edited by Margot O'Keeffe
Printed by Alden Press
ISBN 1-8621-5353-1

For further information about Channel 4 Schools and details of published
materials, contact
Channel 4 Schools
PO Box 100
Warwick CV34 6TZ
Tel: 01926 436444
Fax: 01926 436446

A map of India in Gandhi's time. It was divided into more than 550 small states, each with its own prince.

When Gandhi was about seven years old his father became Prime Minister of another state, Rajkot, and the family moved there. He went to Alfred High School, where he learned English and other subjects.

Like most Hindus, Gandhi was married when he was very young, only 13 years old, to a girl chosen by his parents. He missed a year of school because of the preparations and all the celebrations.

Mohandas Gandhi when he was seven years old.

Did you know?

- *People in India were divided into classes (castes). There were rules about the jobs each caste could do.*

- *Brahmins, the highest caste, were priests and scholars. Next were the Kshatryas: rulers and soldiers.*

- *Gandhi's family belonged to the third caste, the Vaisyas: traders and farmers.*

- *The next lowest caste were the Sudras: manual workers.*

- *Finally, there were the Untouchables, who had dirty jobs such as sweeping streets.*

5

Studying in England

In 1888 Gandhi left school. His eldest brother paid for him to study law in England. A special farewell party was held for him, but he was too shy to say more than a few words.

Before he left home he promised his mother that he would be a good Hindu and not eat meat nor drink wine.

When he was in England he tried to be like the British. He bought English clothes, spending ten pounds on an evening suit, a 'chimney pot' hat and a gold watch on a chain. He had lessons to help him speak English well, play the violin and do ballroom dancing.

Later he realised all this was a waste of time because he would be leaving England in three years to go back home.

Gandhi (on the right) when he was 17 with his elder brother, Laxmidas.

While he was in London, Gandhi kept a note of every penny he spent. He found ways to live more and more cheaply.

He rented a room near where he was training to be a lawyer, so that he did not have to pay fares to get there. He enjoyed finding cheap foods and even learned how to make English meals, like carrot soup.

He read the Hindu holy book for the first time. It said that it was wrong to want to own many nice things. Gandhi agreed with this.

Gandhi finished his training in 1890 and went back to India in June 1891. He was now a lawyer. He had also kept the promise he had made to his mother. He had not eaten any meat nor drunk any wine.

This is a photograph of the Vegetarian Society of England which Gandhi joined. He is the young man in the front row on the left.

Did you know?

- *India was ruled by Britain.*

- *It was unusual for young people from Gandhi's town to go to England to study.*

- *Some people tried to stop him from going because they said the Hindu religion could not be practised there.*

Working in South Africa

When Gandhi arrived back in India he was told that his mother had died. His family had not told him while he was in England because they did not want him to be alone when he heard the sad news.

He found work at the local law courts and, in the next few years, he and his wife had two sons. Then, in 1893, when he was treated badly by a British official, he decided to leave India. He went to South Africa to be a lawyer for a shipping company.

Gandhi's new company had given him a first-class train ticket. In South Africa, people with dark skins were not allowed to travel first class. A white passenger complained about Gandhi being in the first-class carriage, but Gandhi refused to get out because he had a first-class ticket. At the next station the police carried him off the train. He stayed all night in the waiting room.

While Gandhi was working at the law courts, a British official, Charles Ollivant, had Gandhi thrown out of his office.

Next morning, Gandhi sent a telegram to tell his company what had happened. They were very cross and arranged for him to have a first-class compartment in the next train all to himself!

The same thing kept happening to Gandhi in other places. In South Africa, white people did not want to travel with people with dark skins or stay in the same hotels.

On one stagecoach he was forced to sit outside. He agreed because he did not want any more trouble. Then a white man who wanted to smoke outside demanded his seat. When Gandhi refused he was thrown off the coach.

Gandhi made up his mind to change the way in which Indians were treated in South Africa.

Did you know?

- In South Africa people of different races were kept separate in public places like hotels, restaurants, stage-coaches and trains.

- People with dark skins were given the worst of everything.

Fighting for justice

Gandhi called a meeting for all Indians in the town of Pretoria. With their help, he started an organisation which would talk to the authorities about the hardships of the Indian people who lived there. He spoke sincerely and they listened. He was not shy any more!

Gandhi spoke very well for his people. His first success was to persuade the railway authorities to let 'properly dressed' Indians travel first or second class on the trains if they wished to.

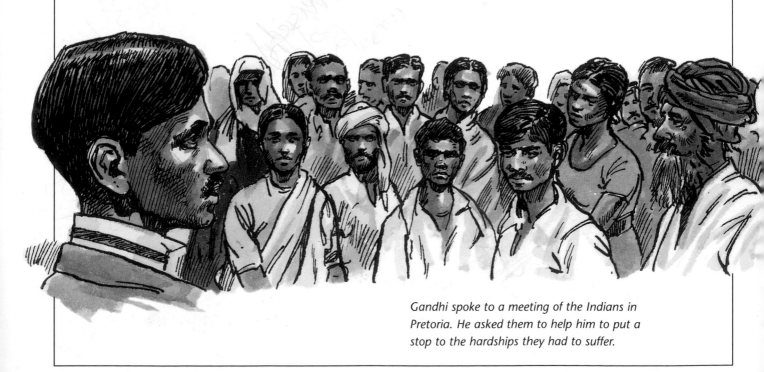

Gandhi spoke to a meeting of the Indians in Pretoria. He asked them to help him to put a stop to the hardships they had to suffer.

Gandhi was about to go home to his family in India when he was told that the South African Government was going to stop Indians from voting in elections. The people asked him to stay and help them to stop this. He stayed for a month to help them but then he left.

In 1896 he went back to South Africa with his wife and children. Some angry Europeans attacked him. He had to stay in a police station for three days for safety.

Gandhi and his family settled down in Durban and their third son, Ramdas, was born in 1897. That year a new law was passed, allowing Indians in South Africa to vote.

Gandhi's wife, Kasturbai, with their sons and a nephew.

Did you know?

- In South Africa, if Indians were found in the streets after 9pm without a pass they were arrested. In some places they were not allowed on the pavements and had to walk in the road!

- It was illegal for Indians to go from one part of the country to another without permission.

Becoming a leader

In 1899 a war began in South Africa, between the Dutch and British people who lived there. To help the British, Gandhi led 1,100 Indians who had trained in the Ambulance Corps. For six weeks, they carried wounded men from the battlefields, sometimes under fire. They often walked as far as 40 kilometres in a day.

At the end of the war Britain gave medals to Gandhi and other members of his Ambulance Corps.

Gandhi took his family back to India in 1901, saying that he would go back to South Africa if he was needed. In 1902 he had to go back again to help Indians who had become refugees after the war. They had not been allowed to go back to their homes.

Gandhi with the Indian Ambulance Corps in 1900.

In 1906 the Government said that all Indians over the age of eight would have to carry a pass with their fingerprints on it. The police could go into their homes at any time and demand to see their pass.

Gandhi held a meeting of more than 3,000 Indians. He told them to say "No" to the new law peacefully. "We may have to go to jail," he said, "We may have to go hungry...some of us may fall ill and die." Everyone there agreed to disobey the new law.

However, these laws had to be passed by the Government in Britain. So Gandhi went to London and talked to some Members of Parliament. They agreed that the law was unfair and it was not passed. Gandhi was very happy.

Gandhi (centre) with his office staff in Johannesburg in 1907. He was still a lawyer.

Did you know?

- *The new law was meant to keep out any more Indian immigrants.*

- *The Indians felt that it was an insult. Because Britain ruled India they were British subjects. They wanted the same rights as other British subjects.*

13

Peaceful protest

The Government of South Africa made a law that only Christian marriages were legal. The Indian women were very upset. They organised a march and were arrested and sent to jail.

Then some Indians who worked in the mines went on strike. Some were turned out of their homes. Gandhi's friends helped by giving food and shelter for the workers and their families.

Gandhi marched 58 kilometres with more than 2,000 men, women and children. He and other leaders of the march were put in prison. The workers were dragged on to trains and taken back to the mines. There they were beaten, but they still refused to work. The Indians did not fight anyone who attacked them.

In 1914 Gandhi talked to the leader of South Africa, who agreed to make changes.

In 1914 Gandhi went home to India. He became the leader of his people. India was still ruled by the British and Gandhi wanted it to be free. He was still a friend to Britain but he wanted India to have its own Government and make its own laws.

There were riots against the British rule and many Indians were hurt. Gandhi wanted them to protest peacefully. Instead of fighting he asked them not to buy any British goods nor to work for anything run by Britain, such as courts, schools and offices.

Thousands of Indians did this but some still fought the British. So Gandhi said he would not eat again until they stopped. He did not eat for a long time and because they loved him and did not want him to die, the people stopped fighting.

Gandhi lived a simple life. He ate very little and wore clothes he had made himself.

Gandhi and his wife wore clothes made from cloth which they spun themselves.

Did you know?

- *In 1919 rioters killed five Europeans, set fire to the town hall, two banks and a railway yard. Then British-led soldiers shot dead hundreds of people at a meeting in Amritsar in the Punjab.*

The 'Salt March'

In March 1930 Gandhi wrote to the head of the British Government in India. He said the laws, especially a new tax on salt, harmed the people of India. He said that, if these laws were not changed, he would lead the people of India to disobey them.

Gandhi set off with some others to march 385 kilometres to the sea, where Indians were no longer allowed to collect salt to sell. He was now 60 years old. More and more people joined the march. Thousands of people broke the law by collecting some salt from the sea.

Police on horseback arrived to stop them. The people lay down on the ground. The police charged, but their horses would not trample the people. So the marchers were carried onto trucks and taken to prison.

Gandhi bent down to pick up some salt. This broke the law.

All around the coasts of India people began to gather salt and to refine it. Hundreds were arrested. Gandhi was sent to prison for six years. He took his spinning-wheel with him.

While he was in prison 2,500 people protested peacefully at a saltworks. Four hundred policemen were sent there to stop them but they did not stop. Suddenly the police charged, beating them with their steel clubs. The marchers fell to the ground. Hundreds had serious injuries and two died.

There were peaceful protests all over India. By June 1930 more than 10,000 Indian protesters were in prison. This did not stop the protests and so, in January 1931, Gandhi and 20 of his people were set free.

The police beat the marchers with sticks.

Did you know?

- *Many people made a living by collecting salt from the sea. The new law stopped them. Now only the Government could collect and sell salt.*

- *The British government put high taxes on alcohol and medicines as well as on salt. Gandhi said that these taxes harmed the poor.*

Success and sadness

Finally, Gandhi and the British made a bargain. The people living near the coast could take salt from the sea for their own use, and the prisoners would be freed from prison. Gandhi told his people to stop the protests.

In December 1931 Gandhi went to London to talk about India ruling itself. The talks did not go well.

Gandhi was unhappy that his own people could be unkind to each other. In 1933 he travelled around India to ask Hindus to treat the lowest caste as their equals. He began to teach the poor people in India how to help themselves.

While he was in London Gandhi went to Buckingham Palace to meet King George V.

In September 1939, World War II began. Britain needed help and Gandhi agreed to give help. In return, he said, Britain must end its rule of India. India finally got its freedom on 15 August 1947.

Gandhi's funeral.

But the Indian people then started to fight one another. There were battles in the streets between Sikhs, Muslims and Hindus. Gandhi was sad because he had wanted them to live together in peace. Once again, he said he would not eat until the fighting stopped. He became very ill and the people stopped fighting.

On 30 January 1948 Gandhi was shot dead by a Hindu who did not agree with what he had done. His funeral procession was more than three kilometres long. Millions of people mourned for Gandhi. Aircraft dropped petals on the procession through New Delhi.

Did you know?

- On 15 August 1947 India was divided into two countries, India for the Hindus and Pakistan for the Muslims.

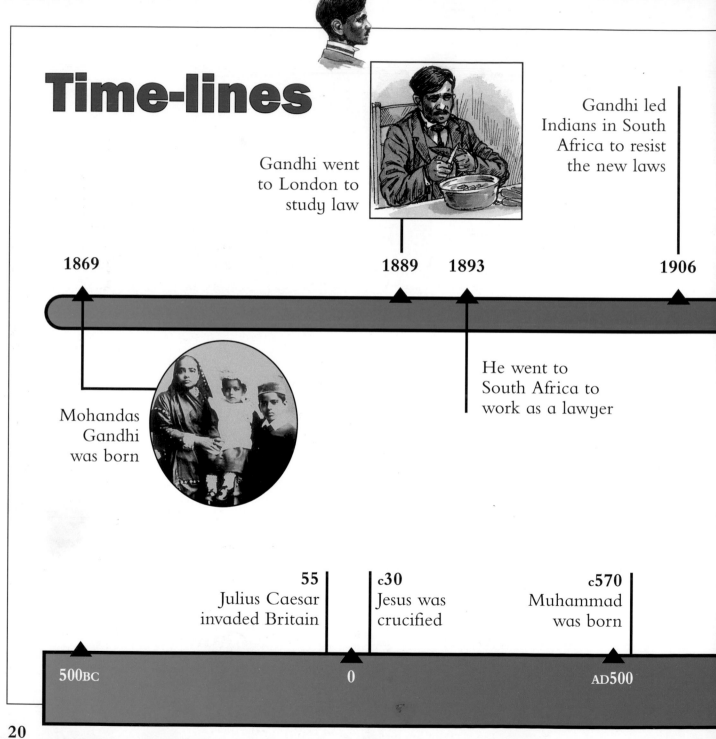

Time-lines

Gandhi went to London to study law

Gandhi led Indians in South Africa to resist the new laws

1869　　　　　　　　　　　1889　1893　　　　　　　　　1906

Mohandas Gandhi was born

He went to South Africa to work as a lawyer

55
Julius Caesar invaded Britain

c30
Jesus was crucified

c570
Muhammad was born

500BC　　　　　　　　　　0　　　　　　　　　AD500

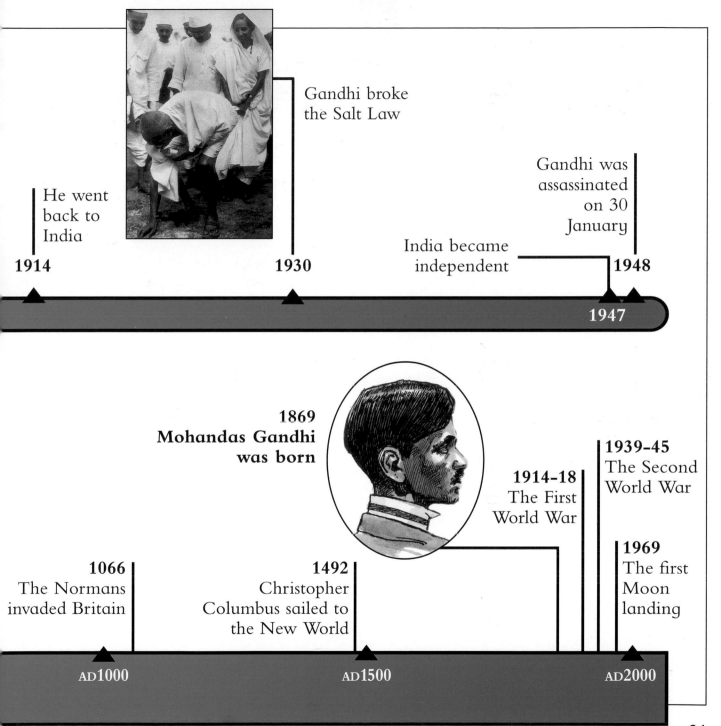

He went
back to
India

1914

Gandhi broke
the Salt Law

1930

India became
independent

Gandhi was
assassinated
on 30
January

1948

1947

1869
Mohandas Gandhi
was born

1939–45
The Second
World War

1914–18
The First
World War

1969
The first
Moon
landing

1066
The Normans
invaded Britain

1492
Christopher
Columbus sailed to
the New World

AD**1000**

AD**1500**

AD**2000**

How to find out more

More books to read

Campaigners for Change by Rosemary Moore (Wayland, 1997)

Gandhi by Peggy Burns (Wayland, 1993)

Mahatma Gandhi by Michael Nicholson (Exley, 1987)

Gandhi by Nigel Hunter (Wayland, 1986)

Mohandas Gandhi by Catherine Bush (Burke, 1985)

CD ROM

Encyclopedia Britannica CD ROM (*Encyclopedia Britannica*, 1998)

The Daily Mail Centenary CD ROM (The *Daily Mail*, 1996)

Places to visit or to which to write

Commonwealth Institute, Kensington High Street, London W8. Tel 0171 603 4535.

Horniman Museum, London Road, London SE23. Tel 0181 699 1872.

Imperial War Museum, Lambeth Road, London SE1. Tel 0171 416 5000.

Indian High Commission, India House, Aldwych, London WC2B. Tel 0171 836 8484.

National Army Museum, Royal Hospital Road, London SW3 4HT. Tel 0171 730 0717.

Glossary

authorities *(10)* People who are in charge of something.

caste *(5)* In India, a group or class into which people are born.

'chimney pot' hat *(6)* A tall silk hat.

corps *(12)* (pronounced 'core') A group of army troops which has a special job.

courts *(8)* Places in which people are put on trial.

disobey *(13)* To break a rule or law.

government *(11)* A group of people in charge of a country.

Hindu *(4)* A person of the Hindu faith.

immigrant *(13)* Someone who moves to a country from somewhere else.

lawyer *(7)* Someone who defends or prosecutes people who have been charged with breaking the law.

legal *(14)* Following the law.

manual workers *(5)* People who work with their hands in jobs such as building roads and railways.

Muslims *(19)* People of the faith founded by the Prophet Muhammad.

prime minister *(4)* Someone who leads the government.

protest *(15)* To act against something with which you disagree.

religious *(4)* Believing in a god and his/her teachings.

Sikhs *(19)* People of the faith founded by Guru Nanak.

subject *(13)* People are subjects of the ruler of their country.

tax *(14)* Money paid to the government of a country by its people.

telegram *(9)* A message sent using electrical wircs, and then printed (without using computers) before faxes or E-mail were invented.

temple *(4)* A building used for worship.

vote *(11)* To choose a government.

Index